BADASS
CIVIL WAR BEARDS

ANNA HIDER AND JULIA HIDER

 John F. Blair, Publisher   *Winston-Salem, North Carolina*

JOHN F. BLAIR,
PUBLISHER

1406 Plaza Drive
Winston-Salem, North Carolina 27103
www.blairpub.com

Printed in Canada

Library of Congress Cataloging-in-Publication Data

Hider, Anna.
  Badass civil war beards / by Anna Hider and Julia Hider.
      pages   cm
  Includes bibliographical references.
  ISBN 978-0-89587-637-9 (alk. paper) — ISBN 978-0-89587-638-6
(ebook) 1. Beards—Pictorial works. 2. Beards—Humor. 3. Sol-
diers—United States—History—19th century—Pictorial works.
4. United States—History—Civil War, 1861-1865—Pictorial works.
I. Hider, Julia. II. Title.
  GT2320.H55 2014
  391.5—dc23

                          2014019017

10 9 8 7 6 5 4 3 2 1

DESIGN BY DEBRA LONG HAMPTON
COVER FONT © IMAGEX

To our family and friends
for being (literal and
metaphorical) "boys."

INTRODUCTION

Four score and seven beards ago . . .

Okay, maybe more like 150 years ago, the Civil War tore America apart. Metaphorically (and sometimes literally), it was brother against brother. It was kind of a big deal at the time and it still is today. America wasn't quite the same afterwards—but everyone knows all about that already.

What most history books fail to mention is the peculiar rise in popularity of ridiculously absurd facial hair. We're talking about completely preposterous, totally out-there stuff. The cause of this phenomenon is still a mystery. Maybe it made the soldiers feel more badass. Perhaps they felt freer to take facial hair risks when they weren't around women. Or did they grow manly beards to strike fear into the hearts of the enemies? Whatever the reason, the trend reached just about everyone—Northerners and Southerners alike sprouted beard, mustache and sideburn styles unlike anything history had ever seen. It was totally awesome.

It's unfortunate that the two sides of this conflict could only see what divided them instead of the facial hair that unified them. But now, we've had a century and a half to reflect on the war, learn from the past, and rediscover this magical Golden Age of Facial Hair.

ACKNOWLEDGMENTS

We probably couldn't have written this book without the help and support of some very awesome people, whom we want to acknowledge right now. First and foremost, we want to thank our family—especially Jim, Jill, Alex (for being a boy), and all of our aunts, uncles, and cousins. Our friends deserve credit as well (especially Katie for her invaluable input on the intro)! We also really, really appreciate everything that everyone at John F. Blair, Publisher, has done for us—Trisina Dickerson, Carolyn Sakowski, Steve Kirk, Debbie Hampton, and everyone else that worked on this book. Additionally, we want to give a shoutout to the people at the Library of Congress for making the process of getting pictures and researching photo permissions so simple. And, last but certainly not least, we want to acknowledge all of our blog's followers and fans—we just want to give a big thanks to each and every one of these beardos for their support.

Robert Byington Mitchell

We're buyington whatever Robert Byington Mitchell is sellington, because that is one hell of a beard.

It's hard not to be im-Preston-ed by A. W. Preston's long mustache. It nearly extends across his entire face.

A. W. Preston
Library of Congress, Civil War Glass Negatives & Related Prints,
LC-DIG-cwpb-05629

'Burns,
baby,
'burns.

Unidentified soldier
Library of Congress, Liljenquist Family Collection of Civil War
Photographs , LC-DIG-ppmsca-34505

Ambrose Burnside:
myth and man,
Sexy sideburns
with him began!

Ambrose Burnside
Library of Congress, Civil War Photographs Collection,
LC-DIG-cwpb-05368

4

Thank God
that's a
Swiss Army knife/
fork/spoon and not
a Swiss Army
razor.

Unidentified soldier

Library of Congress, Liljenquist Family Collection of Civil War Photographs,
LC-DIG-ppmsca-34972

5

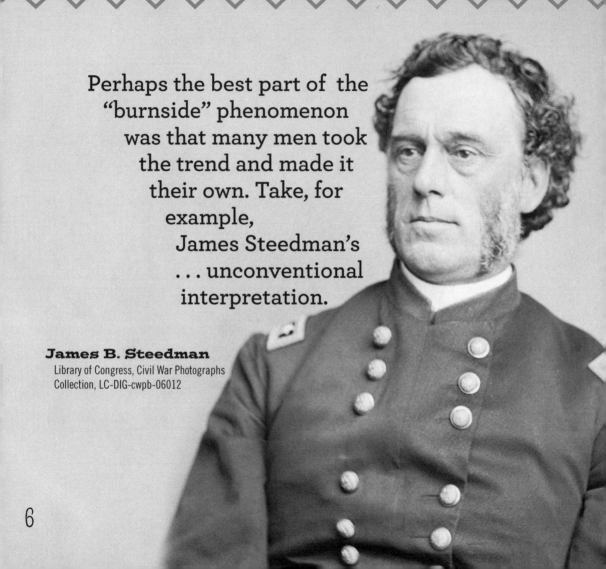

Perhaps the best part of the "burnside" phenomenon was that many men took the trend and made it their own. Take, for example, James Steedman's . . . unconventional interpretation.

James B. Steedman
Library of Congress, Civil War Photographs
Collection, LC-DIG-cwpb-06012

6

This guy has to be part werewolf—there's no other logical, human explanation for his beard.

Unidentified soldier
Library of Congress, Liljenquist Family Collection of Civil War Photographs, LC-DIG-ppmsca-27246

BEARD BATTLE

This is David Wyatt Aiken, who grew kindred beards with his cousin William Aiken.

David Wyatt Aiken

BEARD BATTLE

But William
grew his beard
a hair bigger
(pun intended).

William Aiken
Library of Congress, Brady-Handy Photograph
Collection, LC-DIG-cwpbh-00689

9

This guy's beard is steadily advancing up his face. In a short time, it will take total control.

Unidentified Solider
Library of Congress, Liljenquist Family Collection of Civil War Photographs, LC-DIG-ppmsca-34269

George Ramsey's mustache looks like a tiny pair of white bell bottoms. Groovy.

George Ramsey
Library of Congress, Brady-Handy Photograph Collection, LC-DIG-cwpbh-04368

11

Rear Admiral
John A. Dahlgren's
"burnsides"
appear to be
in ship shape!

John A. Dahlgren
Library of Congress, Brady-Handy
Photograph Collection, LC-DIG-
cwpbh-01153

Friends,
Romeyns,
countrymen . . .
lend me your beard.
Seriously,
Romeyn Ayers,
lend me your beard.
It's awesome.

Romeyn B. Ayres
Library of Congress, Brady-Handy Photograph Collection, LC-DIG-cwpbh-00866

14

Cadmus Wilcox may have been 54th out of 59 students at West Point, but his mustach and sideburns were easily top of the class.

Cadmus Wilcox
Library of Congress, Civil War Glass Negatives & Related Prints, LC-DIG-cwpb-07565

There once was a man named Jackson
Who grew a long beard so flaxen.

He may have been Stony
But his beard wasn't phony—

To all it did bring
satisfaction.

Thomas "Stonewall" Jackson
Library of Congress, Civil War Glass Negatives &
Related Prints, LC-DIG-cwpb-07477

15

Unidentified soldier
Library of Congress, Liljenquist Family Collection of
Civil War Photographs, LC-DIG-ppmsca-27443

Field conditions during the Civil War weren't great. This guy had the right idea by growing "burnsides" that could double as pillows!

Daniel Ullman was a member of the Whig party, which is ironic, because his full, luxurious hair and beard definitely weren't whigs.

Daniel Ullman
Library of Congress, Civil War Glass Negatives & Related Prints, LC-DIG-cwpb-05138

17

John Lennon
actually wasn't the
real Walrus—
Oliver Edwards was.

Oliver Edwards
Library of Congress, Civil War Glass Negatives &
Related Prints, LC-DIG-cwpb-06110

Henry Watterson
Library of Congress, Brady-Handy Photograph Collection,
LC-DIG-cwpbh-05047

Henry Watterson was the editor of a newspaper, and he did a pretty bang-up job of editing that mustache and goatee, too.

19

This guy should forget about drawing maps and stick to growing facial hair.

Unidentified soldier
Library of Congress, Liljenquist Family Collection of Civil War Photographs,
LC-DIG-ppmsca-32133

John Payne Bankhead
Library of Congress, Civil War Glass Negative & Related Prints, LC-DIG-cwpb-06300

John Payne Bankhead was in command of the ironclad ship the USS Monitor when it sank. Unlike the Monitor, his ironclad "burnsides" are UNSINKABLE!

21

George S. Greene had a Greene thumb when it came to beard cultivation. It's like a fantastic topiary of facial hair!

George S. Greene
Library of Congress, Civil War Glass Negatives & Related Prints, LC-DIG-cwpb-05810

Unidentified soldier
Library of Congress, Liljenquist Family Collection of Civil War Photographs, LC-DIG-ppmsca-37263

This guy looks like he's wearing a Santa hat. He probably inspired that famous poem, "The Night Before Beardmas." You know, the one that goes:

'Twas the night before
  Beardmas and all
  through the base,
Not a razor was stirring,
  nor even a face.
The bristled hair hung
  from their chins with care,
With the hopes that
  St. Beardy soon would be
  there.

The most intimidating thing about this photo of Private Thomas Bates isn't that pistol or that knife. It's his big, bad beardy.

Thomas Bates
Library of Congress, Liljenquist Family
Collection of Civil War Photographs
LC-DIG-ppmsca-32600

24

George Crook
isn't a beard crook,
although his beard
is looking a little
crooked.

George Crook
Library of Congress, Brady-Handy Photograph
Collection, LC-DIG-cwpbh-04032

25

Wendell Phillips was a social activist and orator during the Civil War. Some of his favorite causes were abolition of slavery, women's rights, citizenship for Native Americans, and the right to grow your "burnsides" wherever the hell you want on your face.

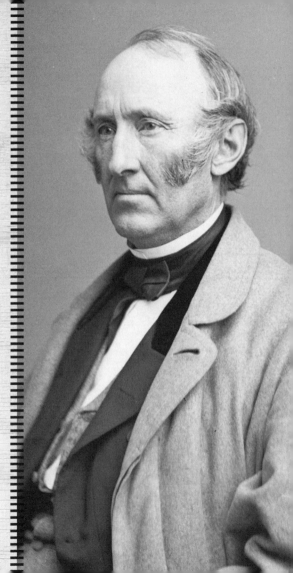

Wendell Phillips
Library of Congress, Brady-Handy Photograph Collection, LC-DIG-cwpbh-01976

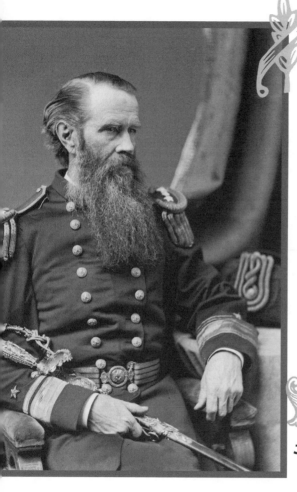

Presenting the
Eighth Wonder
of the World:
"The Hanging Gardens
of John Worden's Face."

John Worden
Library of Congress, Brady-Handy Photograph
Collection, LC-DIG-cwpbh-03896

27

"I like big beards and I cannot lie!"

Albert Jenkins
Library of Congress, Civil War Glass Negatives
and Related Prints, LC-DIG-cwpb-07573

28

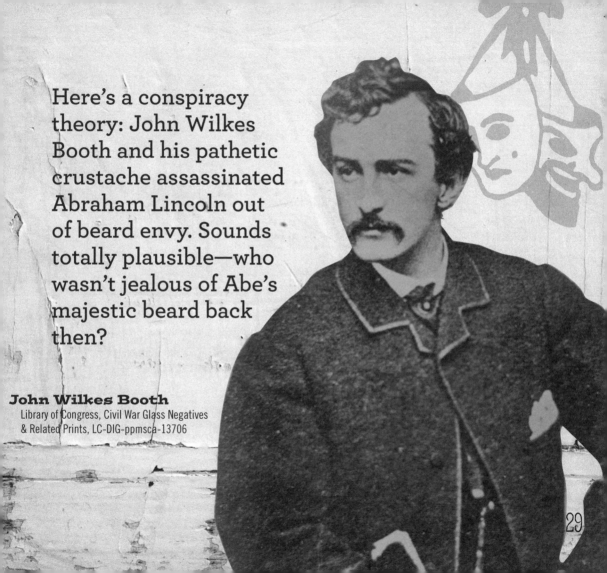

Here's a conspiracy theory: John Wilkes Booth and his pathetic crustache assassinated Abraham Lincoln out of beard envy. Sounds totally plausible—who wasn't jealous of Abe's majestic beard back then?

John Wilkes Booth
Library of Congress, Civil War Glass Negatives
& Related Prints, LC-DIG-ppmsca-13706

29

Vannoy Hartrog Manning
was captured during the
Battle of the Wilderness.
Shaving that beard was also
a battle of the wilderness.

David Dixon Porter brought out the Big Gun for this picture. ("Big Gun" is a nickname for his beard.)

David Dixon Porter
Library of Congress, Civil War Glass Negatives & Related Prints, LC-DIG-ppmsca-34008

31

This guy liked his unibrow so much that he re-created it above his upper lip.

Unidentified soldier

Joseph Warren Revere's grandfather, Paul Revere, may have inspired Henry Wadsworth Longfellow to write a poem about his famous midnight ride, but did you know that there's also a poem inspired by Joe himself? It starts like this:

"Listen my children
and you shall hear
Of the badass beard
of Joe Revere..."

Joseph Warren Revere
Library of Congress, Brady-Handy Photograph Collection, LC-DIG-cwpbh-00757

33

Henry Cornelius Burnett has the body of a linebacker and the face of a pouting toddler. And yet, somehow, he has the beard of a Civil War badass.

Henry Cornelius Burnett
Library of Congress, Brady-Handy Photograph Collection, LC-DIG-cwpbh-02448

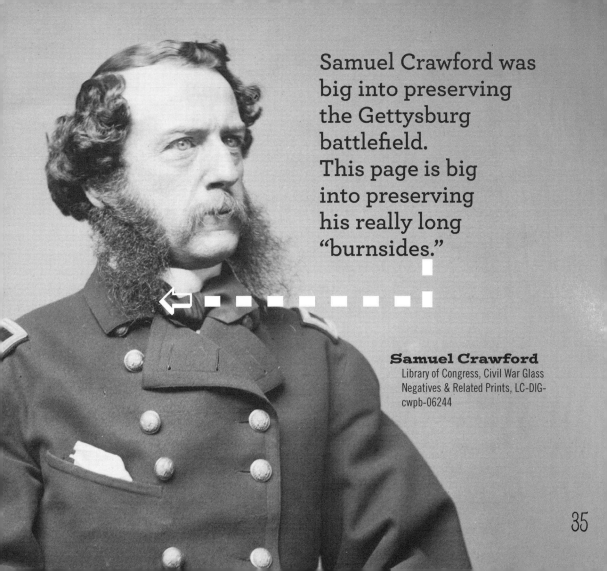

Samuel Crawford was big into preserving the Gettysburg battlefield. This page is big into preserving his really long "burnsides."

Samuel Crawford
Library of Congress, Civil War Glass Negatives & Related Prints, LC-DIG-cwpb-06244

35

Why

the

LONG

face,

John Bell Hood?

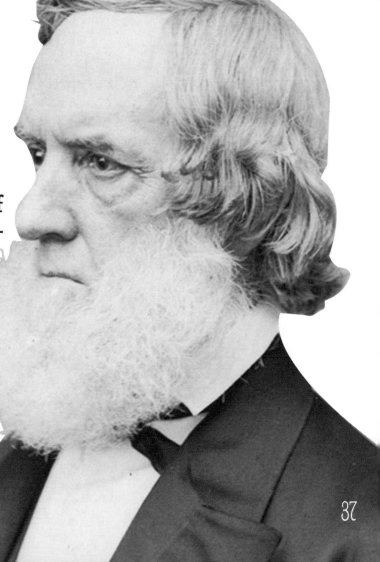

Welles done,
Gideon Welles!
That is by far one of
the fluffiest, softest-
looking beards in
the entire war!

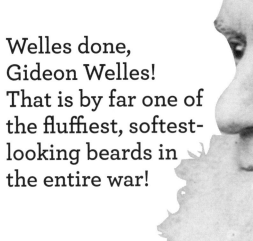

Gideon Welles
Library of Congress, Civil
War Photographs Collection,
LC-DIG-cwpb-04843

37

BEARD BATTLE

This is Edward McCook, of the famed Fighting McCook clan. During the war, they fought Confederates.

Edward McCook
Library of Congress, Civil War Photographs Collection, LC-DIG-cwpb-06228

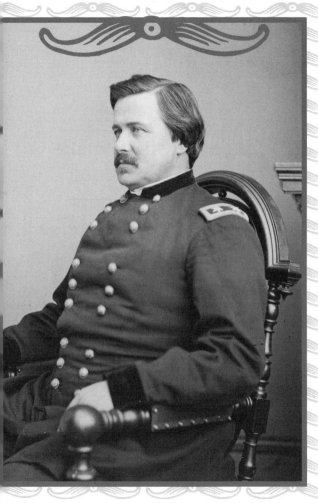

BEARD BATTLE

But now he and his cousin Alexander McCook are going head-to-head in a mustache death match. Maybe their family should have been called the Fighting Mustachioed McCooks.

Alexander McCook
Library of Congress, Civil War Photographs Collection, LC-DIG-cwpb-05611

39

Those specs make Carl Schurz look really intelligent. You know what else makes him look smart? That beard. Because smart people know that beards are the coolest.

Carl Schurz
Library of Congress, Brady-Handy Photograph Collection,
LC-DIG-cwpbh-04020

There are white-collar workers and blue-collar workers. And then there are beard-collar workers. Guess which one this guy is?

Unidentified soldier
Library of Congress, Liljenquist Family Collection of Civil War Photographs, LC-DIG-ppmsca-31685

41

This is Alfred Pleasonton. His mustache is rather Pleasonton, don't you think?

Alfred Pleasonton
Library of Congress, Brady-Handy Photogra[...]
Collection, LC-DIG-cwpbh-00045

What do Roswell Sabine Ripley and Roswell, New Mexico, have in common? They were both visited by aliens. They told Ripley to grow that out-of-this-world beard.

Roswell Sabine Ripley
Library of Congress, Civil War Glass Negatives & Related Prints, LC-DIG-cwpb-06019

43

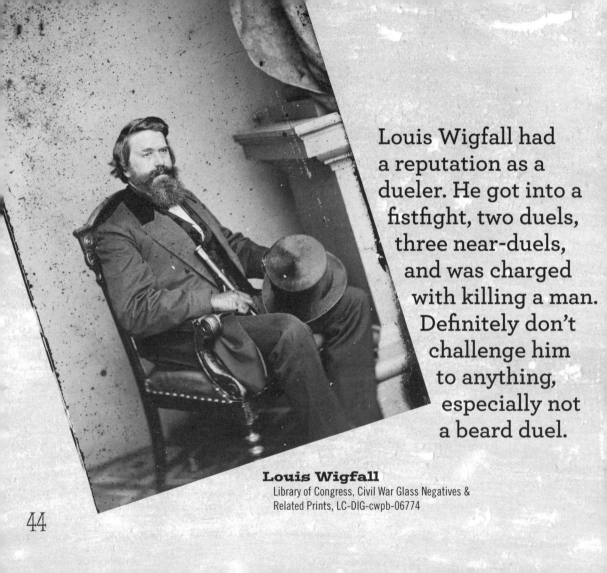

Louis Wigfall had a reputation as a dueler. He got into a fistfight, two duels, three near-duels, and was charged with killing a man. Definitely don't challenge him to anything, especially not a beard duel.

Louis Wigfall
Library of Congress, Civil War Glass Negatives & Related Prints, LC-DIG-cwpb-06774

Jefferson Davis,
Your skunk-tailbeard stinks worse than
This awful haiku.

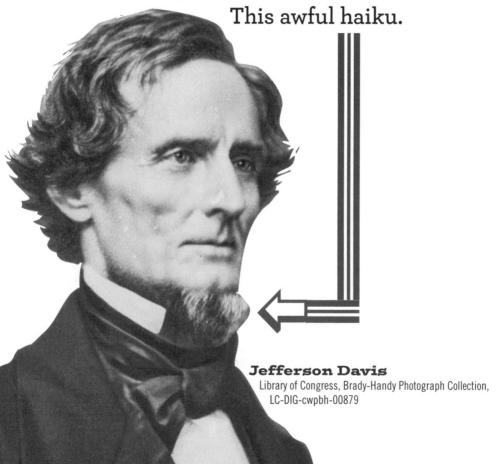

Jefferson Davis
Library of Congress, Brady-Handy Photograph Collection,
LC-DIG-cwpbh-00879

45

See that gold star on George W. Hackworth's belt? The Confederate army gave him that for having such a friggin' sweet beard.

George W. Hackworth
Library of Congress, Liljenquist Family Collection of Civil War Photographs,
LC-DIG-ppmsca-33460

46

James Wadsworth was almost as dedicated to philanthropy (he worked for the army fo' free) as he was to making his "burnsides" into perfect triangles.

James Wadsworth
Library of Congress, Civil War Photographs
Collection, LC-DIG-cwpb-04579

These two tied for first in the Company B beard-growing contest.

Samuel Henry Starr was certainly a beard-growing super Starr. Whoever gave him the nickname "Old Nosebag" was probably just jealous. Every Starr has haters.

Samuel Henry Starr
Library of Congress, Civil War Glass Negatives & Related Prints, LC-DIG-cwpb-04589

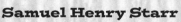

49

General George Pickett may have messed up at Gettysburg, but he sure didn't mess up that goatee.

George Pickett
Library of Congress, Brady-Handy Photograph Collection, LC-DIG-cwpbh-00682

Thomas
Maley
Harris?

More like
Thomas
Manly
Hair-is.

Thomas Maley Harris
Library of Congress, Civil War Glass
Negatives & Related Prints, LC-DIG-
cwpbh-03212

51

Sometimes bigger isn't better. Evidence: Alexander Shaler's whisper-thin mustache.

Alexander Shaler
Library of Congress, Civil War Glass Negatives & Related Prints, LC-DIG-cwpb-05470

Benjamin Sands
Library of Congress, Brady-Handy Photograph Collection,
LC-DIG-cwpbh-00507

ZZZZZZZ

Rear Admiral Benjamin Sands worked part time as The Sandman. But instead of making people fall asleep, he made them grow fab beards like his overnight.

53

Like father, like son? Not quite yet. The kid still has to work on his facial hair—and he has a lot to live up to.

Unidentified soldiers
Library of Congress, Liljenquist Family Collection of
Civil War Photographs, LC-DIG-ppmsca-32139

54

Alexander Webb
Library of Congress, Civil War Photographs
Collection, LC-DIG-cwpb-05917

Alexander Webb
has woven quite
a Webb of facial
hair. A lovely,
tangled webb.

Edwin Stanton
Library of Congress, Brady-Handy Photograph
Collection, LC-DIG-cwpbh-04318

As president, Andrew Johnson fired Secretary of War Edwin Stanton and his magnificent beard and replaced him with a barechin. No wonder Johnson was impeached for the move.

This guy probably used that fife to play popular tunes such as "Battle Hymn of the Beard," "John Brown's Beard," and "Turkey in the Beard."

Unidentified soldier
Library of Congress, Liljenquist Family Collection of Civil War Photographs, LC-DIG-ppmsca-34373

57

Morton C. Hunter
has one mission:
to hunt barechins.

He stalks his prey,
hunting them, until
they grow beards.

Morton C. Hunter
Library of Congress, Brady-Handy
Photograph Collection, LC-DIG-
cwpbh-00498

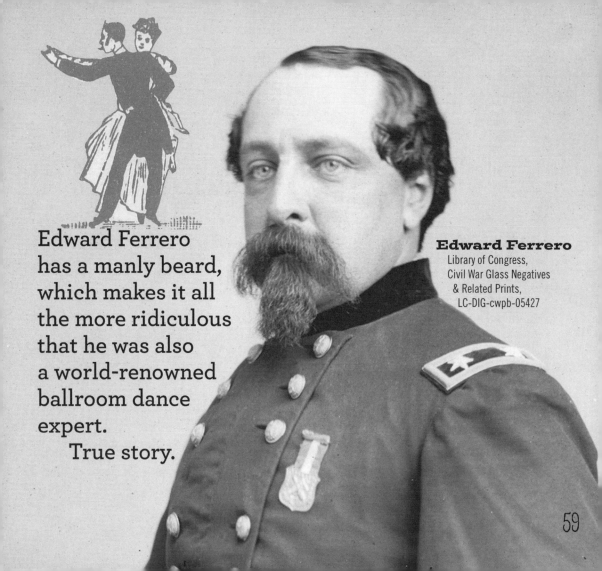

Edward Ferrero
has a manly beard,
which makes it all
the more ridiculous
that he was also
a world-renowned
ballroom dance
expert.
   True story.

Edward Ferrero
Library of Congress,
Civil War Glass Negatives
& Related Prints,
LC-DIG-cwpb-05427

59

William Mahone's soldiers may have called him "Little Billy," but they obviously weren't talking about his enormous beard.

William Mahone
Library of Congress, Brady-Handy Photograph Collection, LC-DIG-cwpbh-04844

Frederick Douglass escaped slavery, traveled the country (and then the world) as a famous abolition-ist orator, produced not one, not two, but FIVE newspapers, fought for women's suffrage, wrote a few autobiographies, was an ambassador, had five kids . . . and he STILL had time to cultivate that stern but glorious beard. A true beardspiration to all!

Frederick Douglass
Library of Congress, Brady-Handy Photograph Collection, LC-DIG-cwpbh-05089

SEAL OF
BEARDSPIRATION

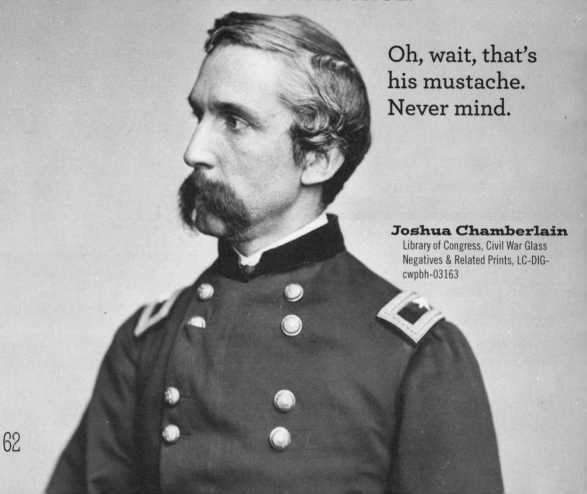

HOLY BEARDHAIRS! JOSHUA CHAMBERLAIN HAS A TARANTULA ON HIS FACE!

Oh, wait, that's his mustache. Never mind.

Joshua Chamberlain
Library of Congress, Civil War Glass Negatives & Related Prints, LC-DIG-cwpbh-03163

Samuel Curtis may have been attempting to grow "burnsides" but he's totally doing it all wrong. The result is surprisingly awesome, though.

Samuel R. Curtis
Library of Congress, Civil War Photographs
Collection, LC-DIG-cwpb-06211

Oh, look! Twin brothers who grew the same style of facial hair. How original! Their other brother clearly looks up to them, though.

Unidentified soldiers
Library of Congress, Liljenquist Family Collection of Civil War Photographs, LC-DIG-ppmsca-37120

The only thing more ridiculous than Beriah Magoffin's name is his beard. Keep in mind that *Beriah Magoffin* is the most ridiculous name of all time.

Beriah Magoffin
Library of Congress, Brady-Handy Photograph Collection, LC-DIG-cwpbh-04512

65

Even though Phil Kearny lost an arm during the Mexican-American War, he was still able to fight in the Civil War (and maintain some really chic facial hair).

Phil Kearny
Library of Congress, Brady-Handy Photograph Collection, LC-DIG-cwpbh-01007

Gabriel Rains is making it rain facial hair. So much better than money. Or actual rain. Or men.

Gabriel Rains
Library of Congress, Civil War Glass Negatives & Related Prints, LC-DIG-cwpb-07530

BEARD BATTLE

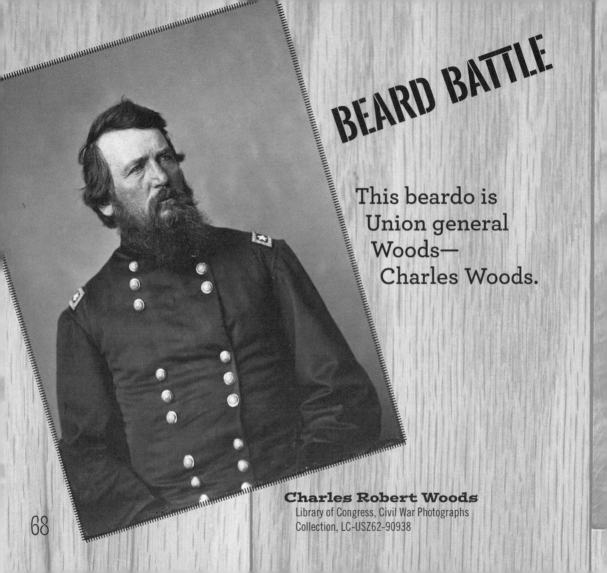

This beardo is
Union general
Woods—
Charles Woods.

Charles Robert Woods
Library of Congress, Civil War Photographs
Collection, LC-USZ62-90938

BEARD BATTLE

And this beardo is Union general Wood—Thomas John Wood. Maybe having a similar last name and a similar job made these two grow equally awesome facial hair.

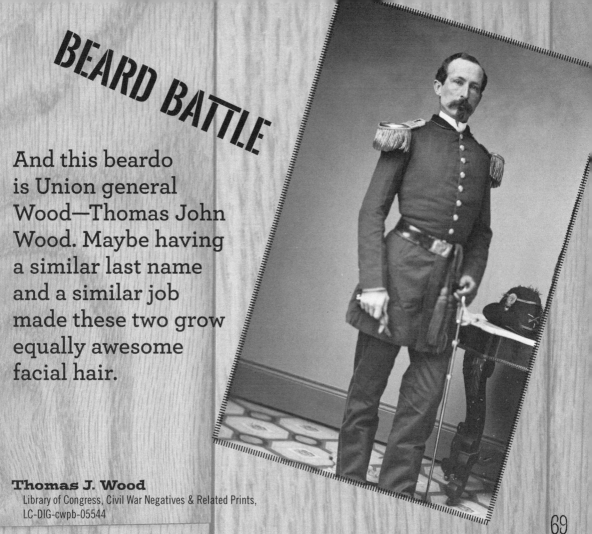

Thomas J. Wood
Library of Congress, Civil War Negatives & Related Prints,
LC-DIG-cwpb-05544

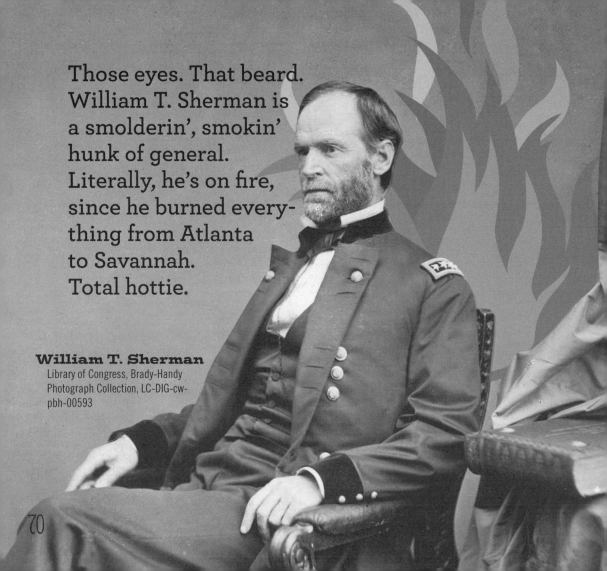

Those eyes. That beard. William T. Sherman is a smolderin', smokin' hunk of general. Literally, he's on fire, since he burned everything from Atlanta to Savannah. Total hottie.

William T. Sherman
Library of Congress, Brady-Handy Photograph Collection, LC-DIG-cw-pbh-00593

70

That is one huge
coat. Hopefully
he has more
beards hidden
underneath it.

Unidentified soldier
Library of Congress, Liljenquist Family
Collection of Civil War Photographs,
LC-DIG-ppmsca-32617

71

Lafayette McLaws was court-martialed for inefficiency during the Civil War. He looks pretty efficient at beard growing, so it must have been about something war-related.

Lafayette McLaws
Library of Congress, Civil War Glass Negatives & Related Prints, LC-DIG-cwpb-07478

John Schofield
was a professor
of experimental
philosophy at
West Point, and
in his spare time
he dabbled in
experimental
beard growing.

John Schofield
Library of Congress, Civil War Photographs Collection, LC-DIG-cwpb-05934

73

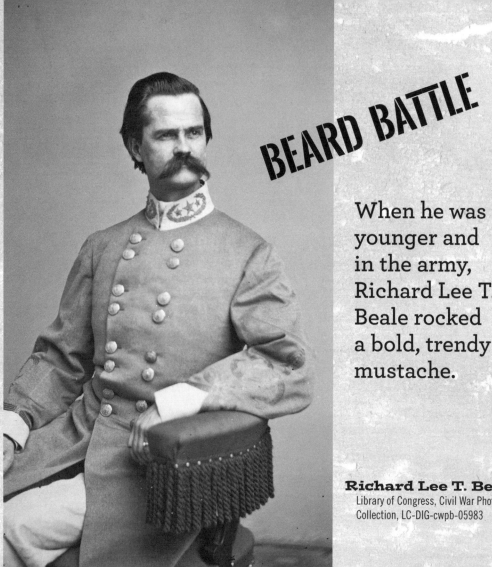

BEARD BATTLE

When he was younger and in the army, Richard Lee T. Beale rocked a bold, trendy mustache.

Richard Lee T. Beale

When he was older, he toned it down and sported a nice, trim beard—presumably the result of a mid-life crisis.

Richard Lee T. Beale
Library of Congress, Brady-Handy Photograph Collection, LC-DIG-cwpbh-04681

Hopefully, these men were careful not to
burn each other's beards off!

Unidentified soldiers
Library of Congress, Liljenquist Family Collection of
Civil War Photographs, LC-DIG-ppmsca-37373

Robert Todd Lincoln is a regular chip off the ol' bearded block. Just like his daddy, Abe!

Robert Todd Lincoln
Library of Congress, Brady-Handy Photograph Collection, LC-DIG-cwpbh-03913

Holy "Burnsides,"
Wade Hampton.

That facial hair style, combined with that outfit, makes this guy look like the neckless wonder. Or the bearded wonder!

Unidentified soldier
Library of Congress, Liljenquist Family Collection of Civil War Photographs, LC-DIG-ppmsca-37144

79

Here's a picture of young Walt Whitman, the famed poet, Civil War nurse, and beard-growing wizard. He's best known for writing "O Captain! My Captain!" Here's an early draft of the poem:

O Beardy! My Beardy! our
   fearful trim is done;
The face has weather'd eve
   rack, the beard we sought
   won;
The mirror is near, the
   water I hear, the barechin
   all exulting,
While follow eyes the barr
   face, the picture grim and
   shaven:
But O beard! beard! beard!
O the facial hairs of gray!
Where on the sink my bear
   hairs lie,
Fallen all astray.

Walt Whitman

With that beard, Fitzhugh Lee Fitz in perfectly with all the other Civil War generals. Maybe being Robert E. Lee's nephew had something to do with it too ...

Fitzhugh Lee
Library of Congress, Brady-Handy Photograph Collection, LC-DIG-cwpbh-03894

81

Kum-beard-ya, my Lord,
kum-beard-ya.

Unidentified soldier
Library of Congress, Liljenquist Family
Collection of Civil War Photographs,
LC-DIG-ppmsca-32132

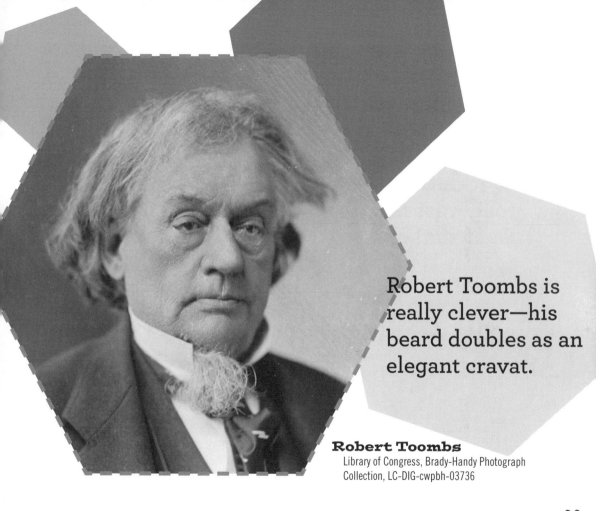

Robert Toombs is really clever—his beard doubles as an elegant cravat.

Robert Toombs
Library of Congress, Brady-Handy Photograph Collection, LC-DIG-cwpbh-03736

This might be the hardest beard battle yet—this is John Cabell Breckinridge, who fought for the Confederacy . . .

BEARD BATTLE

John Cabell Breckinridge
Library of Congress, Civil War Glass Negatives & Related Prints, LC-DIG-cwpb-04791

BEARD BATTLE

. . . and this
is his cousin,
Joseph, who
fought in the
Union army.
At least badass
facial hair runs
in the family.

Joseph Cabell
Breckinridge
Library of Congress, Brady-Handy
Photograph Collection, LC-DIG-
cwpbh-05117

85

Next time he goes to the salon to get his hair done, he should ask his stylist about having his beard done as well.

Unidentified soldier
Library of Congress, Liljenquist Family Collection of Civil War Photographs, LC-DIG-ppmsca-37075

Richard Ewell's nickname may have been *"Old Bald Head,"* but perhaps "Old Beard Face" would have been more appropriate.

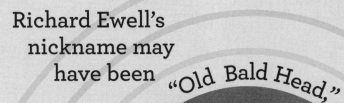

Richard Ewell
Library of Congress, Civil War Glass Negatives & Related Prints, LC-DIG-cwpb-07437

You know what's more impressive than that huge knife? The fact that this guy used it to shave his face.

Unidentified soldier
Library of Congress, Liljenquist Family Collection of Civil War Photographs, LC-DIG-ppmsca-32623

James Madison Leach
Library of Congress, Brady-Handy Photograph Collection, LC-DIG-cwpbh-04648

James Madison Leach's beard is so natural and wild and free. Like the mane of a wild stallion as it gallops unbridled across the plains.

89

Hamilton Fish
never had to Fish
for compliments
with that glorious
facial hair.

Hamilton Fish
Library of Congress, Brady-Handy Photograph Collection,
LC-DIG-cwpbh-00906

90

Excuse me, young man. How old are you? And where did you get that mustache? You don't look like you're old enough to have that.

Unidentified soldier
Library of Congress, Liljenquist Family Collection of Civil War Photographs, LC-DIG-ppmsca-27296

Alpheus S. Williams's beard is the alpheus and the omega of beards. It is the first and the last, the end-all and be-all of beards.

Alpheus S. Williams